From Milk
to Yoghurt

A RECIPE FOR LIVING & DYING

Ringu Tulku Rinpoche

Bodhicharya
PUBLICATIONS
Awaken the heart by opening the mind

First Published in 2009 by
BODHICHARYA PUBLICATIONS
24 Chester Street, Oxford, OX4 1SN, United Kingdom.
www.bodhicharya.org   email: publications@bodhicharya.com

Text & calligraphy ©2009 Ringu Tulku

Printed on recycled paper by Imprint Digital, Devon, UK.

ISBN 978-0-9534489-7-5
Second Edition. 2013

Rebirth: transcribed by Maria Huendorf, edited by Marita Faaberg, Margaret Ford, Ringu Tulku and the Bodhicharya Publishing team.

Working with a Spiritual Teacher: transcribed by Cait Collins, edited by Marita Faaberg, Margaret Ford, Ringu Tulku and the Bodhicharya Publishing team.

Death and Dying: transcribed by Claire Trueman, edited by Marita Faaberg, Margaret Ford, Ringu Tulku and the Bodhicharya Publishing team.

Typesetting, design and photography by Paul O'Connor at Judo Design, Ireland.

Calligraphy by Ringu Tulku:
Transformation (opposite), *Rebirth* (page 4), *Devotion* (page 20), *Bardo* (page 38).

Front Cover Photo: ©Paul Hocksenar
Back Cover Photo: ©Paul O'Connor

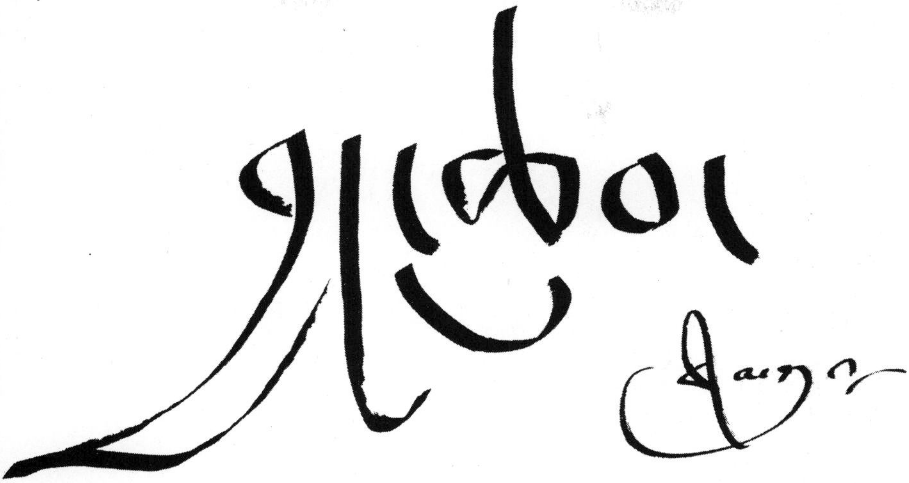

Editors' Preface

With many thanks for the hard work and dedication of the Bodhicharya Publications team including Marita Faaberg, Claire Trueman, Mary Heneghan, Eric Masterton, Tim Barrow, Minna Stenroos, Jet Mort, Maria Huendorf, Annie Dibble, Rachel Moffit, Dave Tuffield. This has been our first 'team' effort and it was a joy to work with them all. Also, Peter Ford, our hidden member of the publishing team. His love, support and encouragement, are the driving forces behind everything I do.

With enormous gratitude to Paul O'Connor for his beautiful layout and design and his kind patience.

With thanks and appreciation to the Theosophical Society Glasgow, the Bodhicharya Buddhist Group Sussex and to Bodhicharya London, who organised the talks included in this book.

With special thanks and love to Ringu Tulku for sharing his heart wisdom that is contained in this book. May it benefit everyone who reads it.

Margaret Ford
Bodhicharya Publications
June 2009

Contents

Introduction

The idea behind the Heart Wisdom Series of books is to make more widely available the vast number of talks and teachings given by Ringu Tulku Rinpoche. Ringu Tulku has travelled extensively around the world since 1990, giving teachings and participating in seminars in Dharma centres, universities, village halls, cinemas, wherever he was invited. Most of these talks have been recorded and are stored in his archive in Hamburg.

This book contains three separate adapted and edited public talks given by Ringu Tulku over a number of years. "Rebirth" was given in Glasgow, Scotland in 1995; "Working with a Spiritual Teacher" in Sussex, England in 1999 and "Death and Dying" in London, England in 2008.

If you have attended a talk or teaching given by Ringu Tulku you will know that his style is gentle and relaxed with much humour. But Rinpoche is a Professor of Tibetology and has received teachings and training from many of the most realised and compassionate teachers from Tibet, such as His Holiness the 16th Gyalwa Karmapa and His Holiness Dilgo Khyentse Rinpoche. His public talks use an apparent simplicity of expression to explain the most profound Buddhist philosophies.

You will also see from these talks that Rinpoche invites many questions. He has said often "It's not good for just one person to talk too much!", and we have included here Rinpoche's dialogue with his audience. Whilst you read, you may have more questions; as it's not expected that you will understand or accept all the points put forward in these few pages.

There are many avenues to explore these. For example, we would like to point out the forums for further study and discussion set up on the Bodhicharya website (www.bodhicharya.org). There is also information here about local study and meditation groups and a schedule for the talks and teachings Rinpoche continues to give around the world.

Margaret Ford and Mary Heneghan

Bodhicharya Publications

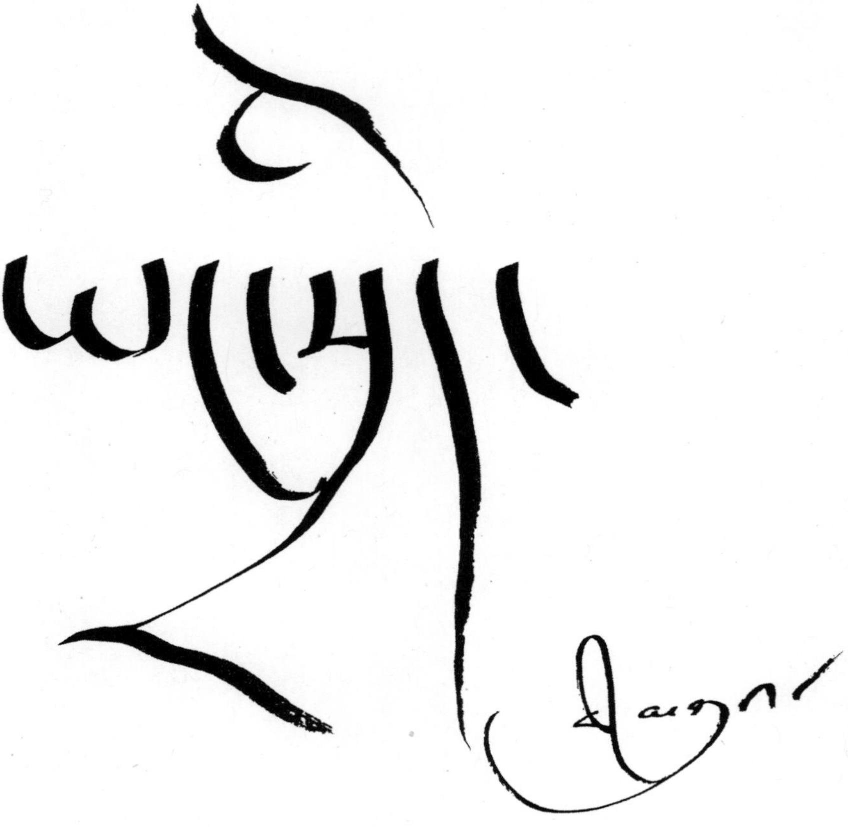

Rebirth: A Buddhist View

I don't think that I would be able to prove to you that there is such a thing as rebirth but I would like to go into some of the Buddhist understanding. This idea is something that exists in almost all spiritual traditions, but in the west there seems to be some resistance in accepting it. Maybe this is just a cultural thing, and perhaps it is gradually changing, but for a long time to talk about rebirth was considered to be like a fiction, something akin to story-telling.

Rebirth is rather difficult to understand. It is not something directly seen with our eyes, nor is it something that can be tested in a laboratory. But if you look more closely at yourself, you have this feeling, this understanding, and a kind of experience of existing not only for a short period. When you look at this feeling deeply, without any prejudice, without any assumptions, really open yourself deep down and try to experience this feeling, I think most people would sense that we are not just here for a short time. You can see and feel, maybe understand, that the life that you have now is not just a single life with nothing before it and nothing afterwards.

Rebirth has been a question of debate for centuries in Buddhism. The Pramanavartika is a book on Buddhist logic and dedicates almost half of its contents to this topic. It includes debates about whether there is an afterlife or not. But I learned the hard way that one cannot convince anybody about anything through debate alone. When I was young I thought that if you could prove something through logic, then everybody would be convinced. This happens when you are young and hot-blooded. Fortunately one becomes wiser with age.

Interdependence

When we think about rebirth, the most important principle in Buddhist philosophy is interdependence. The true nature of everything is interdependence. This means that everything, any entity in the whole universe, be it mental, material or whatever, cannot be found to be just one thing - an entity completely independent or permanent. Everything is compounded, or made up of many elements. Each element is dependent on all others, and every one of them is also impermanent. Therefore any compounded entity is impermanent.

Anything that is caused by many other things is therefore interdependent. If one single cause or condition were to be missing, the whole thing would disappear. But when the different elements that are needed for something to happen are there, then it appears. So, although you can see many things as existing, they have no intrinsic existence of their own. Everything flows. Whatever we are, whatever I am now, is caused by the previous moment. And the previous moment was caused by the one before that.

Taking this to a more gross level, the cause of this present life was the previous life, and the previous life was caused by the life before that. When we express it in these terms, we are talking at a very simple level. But actually when we talk about a deeper theory of rebirth, we are not talking about just the change from one life to the next, because the actual change does not happen as in a series of blocks, this change takes place constantly. What I am at this moment is not just because of my past life, it is also because of all my life until now. I have changed so much since I was born, you would have not recognized me then. When I was ten or fifteen years old I was not this bad to look at! What I am now is a result of all my past since I was born, and since before my birth. This change is taking place every moment, and it is both an external and an internal change. It is not only my consciousness that changes; it is the external interdependent conditions, as well as the internal conditions. My consciousness, the causes and conditions, all of these keep changing continuously, and each cause creates an effect on the next moment of my life.

The first thing we must understand is that rebirth, like everything else, is interrelated, and that in order to really understand the theory of rebirth, you have to understand your true nature, how you really are. If we do not truly understand the way we are in ourselves, we will not be able to understand rebirth fully. The way we are is not something solid. We are not just one substantial unchangeable thing.

When we think about rebirth, we generally come to believe that when we die, our soul or consciousness comes out of our body, and then it takes on another body. That is not the Buddhist point of view; it is not like changing clothes. You don't just take off these clothes, this body, and then you put on new clothes, a new body. It is not like that. The relationship between mind and body is much closer, very intricate, it is almost inseparable. In addition, the physical components of the body you have now, causes something new to come up. In the same way, the present consciousness also causes some other consciousness to come up.

Take for example my mind now. How do you know I was here yesterday and not elsewhere? How can we prove that? Many of you did not see me yesterday. How can you definitely say that I was here yesterday? I may be an E.T, an extraterrestrial being, I look a little bit like it! Or I may just have popped up from under the ground. Nothing is for sure. Nevertheless, you can be sure that I was here yesterday, because I am here now. My existence here now is the proof that I was also here yesterday. In the same way you have proof that I was here the day before yesterday because I was present yesterday. The proof of my being here yesterday is my being here now; and the proof of my being here tomorrow would also be my being here at this moment now. Tomorrow I may or may not be here. Nevertheless, I will be somewhere because I am here now. I would not just completely disappear. I could die maybe, but even then, that would not mean the end of everything. Everything dies and again comes up, that is the nature of things. There was a spring last year and it went away, but then it has come back again this year. The sun has gone down today but it will come up tomorrow because it was here today. It is the law of nature that nothing completely stops, that everything causes something else to appear, and that, in turn, causes something else. So it is this continuous cause and effect that is referred to when we talk about rebirth. The law of cause and effect is what the rebirth theory is based on.

Next Life Yoghurt

In the Buddhist concept of rebirth, lives are not seen as different beads on one string, each bead being a life which continues life after life, strung to the soul on a long thread. It is not like that. There are five different examples that are traditionally given to explain this further: yoghurt; a recitation; a mirror; a seal and lastly a lamp.

Let's take the first example of yoghurt. How do you make yoghurt? It is with milk, but is milk yoghurt? No. Is yoghurt milk? It is not. But without milk we do not have yoghurt. And can we say that yoghurt is the same substance as the original milk? Again no, it is not the same. In a similar manner, our next life or the next moment of change, when we move from one place to another, from one instant to the next or from one life to another, it happens in a similar way. What I am now is not exactly my next life; it is different like the yoghurt. Now I am milk, but in the next life I may become yoghurt!

Now the examples of recitation and mirror are similar. If I recite a sutra you will hear it, but nothing goes from me to you. I don't take the sutra from me and throw it to you so you can have it, but still you all get it. Also a mirror; when I stand in front of a mirror you and I can see I am there in the mirror, but I am not really in the mirror. Nothing has gone from me into the mirror, but without me and the mirror there would be no reflection.

Then there is the seal. In the olden days a wax seal would be used to seal important letters from a king, or someone important. But what goes from the original seal to the seal on the letter? It is an impression only, but still it is the seal, although not the original one.

The lamp is one of the better known examples. Perhaps you have heard the story of King Milinda and his questions? It is a very important book in Buddhism, a very nice book, very interesting. It has been translated into English also. Milinda was a Greek king, he ruled in the Kashmir area of India. At that time there was an Indian scholar-saint named Nagasena. The king invited him and asked him many questions such as, "How do these changes take place, how does this life continue into another life and then becomes a rebirth?" Nagasena answered in this way: "Nothing goes from here to there." But how could that happen? He went on to say: "Suppose you lit a candle or a butter-lamp, how long will it last? Well, the butter-lamp may last all night, if it is a big one. The flame you had at the beginning, the flame that continues throughout the night, and the flame at the end of the night, is it the same flame or not? It has been burning continuously from the moment the lamp was full, through all the different hours of the night, and then there was only a small part of the lamp left. Could it be one and the same flame? It has been burning continuously throughout the night, so you cannot say that it is just one flame. It is a continuation of a flame. But at the same time you cannot say that it is different, because it is the same flame."

The Continuous Flow

Cause and effect work like this. This moment's consciousness is the cause of the next moment of consciousness and that is the cause of the next.

And when I die, at that time, it is not that my body dies and my mind goes somewhere else; the process is the same: the body disintegrates, and also the mind dies. From the Buddhist point of view we say that all mental factors - mind, emotions and all this - cease, and out of that something else comes up. For example, every time a thought comes up and goes, the next thought comes up. And out of that, there arises yet another thing. Something is always taking place, a continuous flow.

When all of our conscious mental factors die, a new set of mental factors arise because of cause and effect. When we die, there is a state we call bardo, the in-between state. At that time we are not a single mind but a complex aggregate. At this point we do not have a material physical body as we do now, but we have a mental body. One moment continues into another, one moment changes into the next. In this way the whole process never stops. Rebirth is this continuity. It is not the continuation of one "thing"; it is a continuation of many things. The cause now is not exactly the ensuing result but the result cannot come unless the cause is there. The relationship between past and present and present and future is very strong. They are interdependent. Because of this state now, the next state arises. The next state cannot be there unless this state is also here. And yet, it is not exactly the same.

Karmapa

The recognition of a Tulku, the recognition of a rebirth, is very Tibetan. The concept was also accepted in India, but the recognition of the rebirth of Lamas, from one life to the next, more or less started in Tibet.

Maybe you know this story about the Karmapa? In the 12th Century in Tibet, there was one Lama who later came to be called Karmapa. He was told by his teacher that he must build three monasteries, two in Kham and the third one in central Tibet near Lhasa. During his life, Karmapa built the two monasteries in Kham, and when he was around eighty years old he told his students: "I must go and build the third monastery I promised my guru." So, although he was very old, he travelled to central Tibet. There he built a little hut, but then he died. But before he died, he said: "Do not dismantle any of the things I have done, and do not give away my books and other things, but keep them. I will come back."

After a few years a small child appeared and said, "I am Karmapa." So, everyone said, "Alright, you are Karmapa!" He was then trained over time by Lamas of different traditions and he turned out to be an extraordinary person. He stayed with the Sakyapa Lamas, who at the time were very famous. Maybe you have heard about the adventures of Marco Polo in Kublai Khan's time where these Tibetan lamas used to make and stop rain, or make a cup come up to your lips unaided? It was the second Karmapa who was supposed to have done these things. The Karmapa served as Chogyal Phagpa's ritual master for some time and travelled to Mongolia and China with him. Chogyal Phagpa was the first Tibetan Lama to rule Tibet. Later, the second Karmapa became the teacher of the Mongolian Kings and, by the time of his death, he had become very famous.

The third Karmapa was recognized by a student of the second Karmapa, the student's name was Urgyenpa. He was a highly regarded Lama who went to India many times, a great sage and scholar. When the third Karmapa was still in his mother's womb, Urgyenpa said: "Your child will be born a boy, and he will be the rebirth of Karmapa." And when the child was born, Urgyenpa declared: "This is Karmapa." This was the first time in Tibetan history, maybe in the history of the world, that a certain child was recognized by another person as being the rebirth of a previous person. This child was very special. When he grew up he remembered everything about his past, and not only that, he also remembered all his experiences in his mother's womb. He actually wrote an autobiography about his time in his mother's womb!

The institutionalisation of recognising rebirths began in Tibet. Other important Lamas, like the Dalai Lamas and the Panchen Lamas, were also recognised, and now there are countless recognitions. When a Lama who had many students and, in particular, has died a good death, with signs of spiritual attainment, then a rebirth was always quickly sought. They found small children whom they trained very well for many years. People in Tibet respect these Tulkus, as they are known, and so far they enjoy a good reputation.

Questions & Answers

Student: How do you explain the growth of world-population, now there are so many more people in the world?

Rinpoche: There is a very good reason for that. In Buddhism we do not believe that this earth is the only place inhabited by different beings. The sphere in which beings can be born is almost limitless. As far as there is space, there can be life. Perhaps I shouldn't say this, because sometimes I make things more complicated and confusing than need be. Once in the south of France, I was asked to give a series of talks on the different Buddhist philosophies, the mind investigation of different philosophies, and I was talking a lot. After the course had finished one woman came up and said: "Well, when you first started talking, it was all so interesting that I bought all your tapes. When I was listening to the tapes, on the first tape I understood everything, the second tape was alright, the third tape was terrible, and by the fourth tape I did not understand anything. It was all too much. I was totally confused, so I took the whole thing and threw it out of the window."

Anyway, I will say it, and you can take it or leave it. You have heard that the Buddhists have a term they call emptiness, known as Shunyata. It is one of the main philosophies of Buddhism. What do we mean by emptiness? Actually emptiness and interdependence are just one and the same thing. When we talk about emptiness, we mean to say that when you analyse anything at all you can think of, you find that it is made of many things, caused by many things. A glass, for example, if you break it down to its parts, it is made of particles, they are made of atoms, and the atoms are made of neutrons and electrons, and so it goes on. It all goes into some kind of energy. Scientists call it the quantum theory.

The traditional Buddhist way of debating this point is to investigate the smallest thing to be found. Any amount of matter must be made of the tiniest of particles and should be able to disintegrate into the tiniest of things. Buddhists call this the partless particle, and say that everything must be made of partless particles. Now another philosopher asked about the nature of this partless particle. Does it have an upper side and a lower side, and an Eastern side and Western side? If we say that it does not have any sides, how is it able to have an effect on anything? And if it can be further divided, it cannot be partless. If it is really partless, it would be almost nothing.

That is the source, the starting point of everything. In the real sense, we come to the conclusion that everything is made of nothing. We say that everything has an unborn quality, an unborn nature. It is but an appearance, seemingly there because of the different causes and effects. And in the same manner, causes and effects also appear, but have no substance.

In this way, a whole universe can exist in one speck of dust. Because it appears out of nothing it does not need any space to accommodate it. And a whole kalpa exists in one moment. Time and space are just relative. There is nothing absolute about time and space. With this understanding there can be another universe in my little finger, the whole population of the world might be coming out of my little finger!

Student: Is it your choice where you go when you are reborn?

Rinpoche: Yes and no. Here is where we talk about karma. Karma is very important in order to understand rebirth and anything else. First one has to understand that what I am now is the result of my karma, of my past. It is not just past lives, it is also of all my life this time, now. What I did yesterday, what I did last year, how I got educated, how I met different people. Everything up to now is the previous cause of what I am right now. What I am now is the result of my karma. Whatever I am at this moment, whether I hate myself or not, or want to be who I am or not. I cannot do anything to change that. I am what I am.

But from this moment onwards, the future is open to me. Within the limits of my past, within the limitations of my present, whatever I am, I can change. Instead of doing what I'm doing now, I can stop and do something else. I can go out, whatever I like, I have many different possibilities. I cannot fly, it is not in my body to fly. I have not done enough yoga! Maybe if I had I would be able to fly, but since I have not done so, I cannot do it.

There are four kinds of results which depend on karma. The strongest action has the most immediate reaction, the most immediate result. Certain karmas are not very strong so the reaction might come later in this life or in the next life. There are even weaker karmas, the result of which might come many lives from now. There are also karmas which may not come at all.

When we talk about the bardo state, we are actually talking about four intermediate states. The first one is called the bardo of life (Tibetan: chewa bardo). It is this life now; we consider that also as a bardo, a very important opportunity. The most important time is now, when we are alive.

Then there comes the bardo of dying (Tibetan: chikai bardo). It starts at the moment when the five elements of our body begin to disintegrate up to the moment when we are declared medically dead.

Then there is the bardo of luminosity (Tibetan: chōnyi bardo). When you die, there comes a very short state where all your concepts, all your mental factors dissolve. Then you see the clear light, your true nature, the basic ordinary essence of being. At that time, if you recognize this as the bardo of luminosity, all illusion stops. There are no more cycles in samsara, no more delusions. You are no longer trapped in karmic conditioning and you become free from all conditioning.

If you do not realise that then the next bardo arises. In this bardo you have a mental body, as I mentioned before, and you are also able to reach whatever place you want. Because you have no body to carry, you can think of London or New York and you are immediately there. You can travel at the speed of thought. You can see through time and space and it could be said that, at this point, you have lots of power.

Nevertheless, depending on your own past and present state of mind, you can also be very afraid. You can feel very insecure. So you search for some security, something to hold on to. That is how you take on another life form (Tibetan: sipa bardo).

If at that time you realise you are in that state and if you have had some meditation training in this life, you can stabilize your mind by saying to yourself: "Whatever is happening at this moment, whatever I see, this is just a mental state. There is no security anywhere, anyway. Nothing and no one can hurt me, so there is no need to fear. I no longer have a body, I am completely free." In this way you become fearless and calm. When there is no fear, there is no agitation either. When there is no agitation, fear, attachment and aversion are also absent. You can choose whatever you want to do, wherever you want to go. You are free. You can take on whatever life form you desire.

But most often, because of too much fear, your mind becomes very unstable and you grasp at whatever comes along. You seem to have no choice. But if you are clear enough in your mind, and stable enough in your attitude, you will be able to make choices. It is not that you are assigned to become something out of compulsion. But because of our previous conditioning, and habitual patterns, we can call it our karmic influences, we usually follow the patterns we are used to. Our habitual patterns make all of us do the same thing again and again. We tend to repeat the same mistakes.

Student: When you first became aware of being the reincarnation of someone, what kind of memory or consciousness did you have of previous lives?

Rinpoche: I do not even remember when I was first recognized as a reincarnated Lama. I was very small. I do not have any memories of my past lives. I do not even have much remembrance of yesterday! Sometimes I hold my pen in this hand, and search for it all over, not remembering I'm holding it!

Student: Is there in Buddhism, faith or belief in a time lapse between the death in this world and the amount of time you will remain in the interval before you come back. Does it happen quickly, or has there to be a certain lapse of time to gather yourself together?

Rinpoche: It is not a fixed, definite thing. Usually people say seven weeks. For seven weeks, after death there are pujas, ceremonies and practices conducted, but it is not definite.

Student: What is the origin of all these things? How did all these things come to be what they are?

Rinpoche: This is a very complex question. This question is asked all the time in many different forms by innumerable people: Where do things come from in the first place? What came first? People asked this very same question of the Buddha. Where does everything come from? What was the first thing to appear? How did it happen? They asked whether a god created it, or who created god, whether he was eternal or not. And the Buddha said: "I do not want to answer this question. It is no use trying to answer this question."

And the reason he did not want to answer is because these fundamental questions are based on wrong assumptions. Where does it all come from? Does it come from something or from nothing? If you say it comes from something, then where does that something come from? And so on. Now, if you say it comes from nothing, how did that nothing come to be? How can nothing change into something? What is the nature of that nothing? You can go on and on and there is never an end to it.

What Buddha was saying is that if you follow this kind of reasoning you will never arrive at a definite answer because you are asking a question based on a wrong premise. What is the real nature of things? We must find out first what is the nature of everything we see, feel and experience. When you see the true nature of things directly, this question will dissolve by itself. You will understand then where everything comes or does not come from. The Buddha continued in this way: "Whether you talk about mind or matter; what is the true nature of these things?" We enter now into the philosophy of Shunyata, the philosophy of interdependence. If everything is unborn in its true nature, then everything appears but there is no solid reality to any of it. Then the question: "Where does it all come from?" does not arise in the first place.

But then again another question arises: Well, alright, the true nature is unborn, Shunyata, interdependence. But we do not see things in this way. How did we ever get this deluded? Now again it is the same thing: What do you mean by you getting deluded? Who are you? Who am I? Upon seeing the true nature of who I am, who you are, you will realise that you have never been deluded.

There is the term of a "gateless gate". You will see wisdom when you have passed through the gateless gate. What is the nature of this gateless gate? Once you have passed through it, you will realise that there has never been a gate at all. When you understand this, when you realise what you really are, then you will come to know that there has never been any delusion.

Student: Is there an infinite series of universes, or is everything there all the time anyway?

Rinpoche: Maybe you can put it that way, you can have a conceptual understanding of it, and you could be right. You can talk about it in many different ways, and you could be wrong also. It is quite complicated, or very simple in a way.

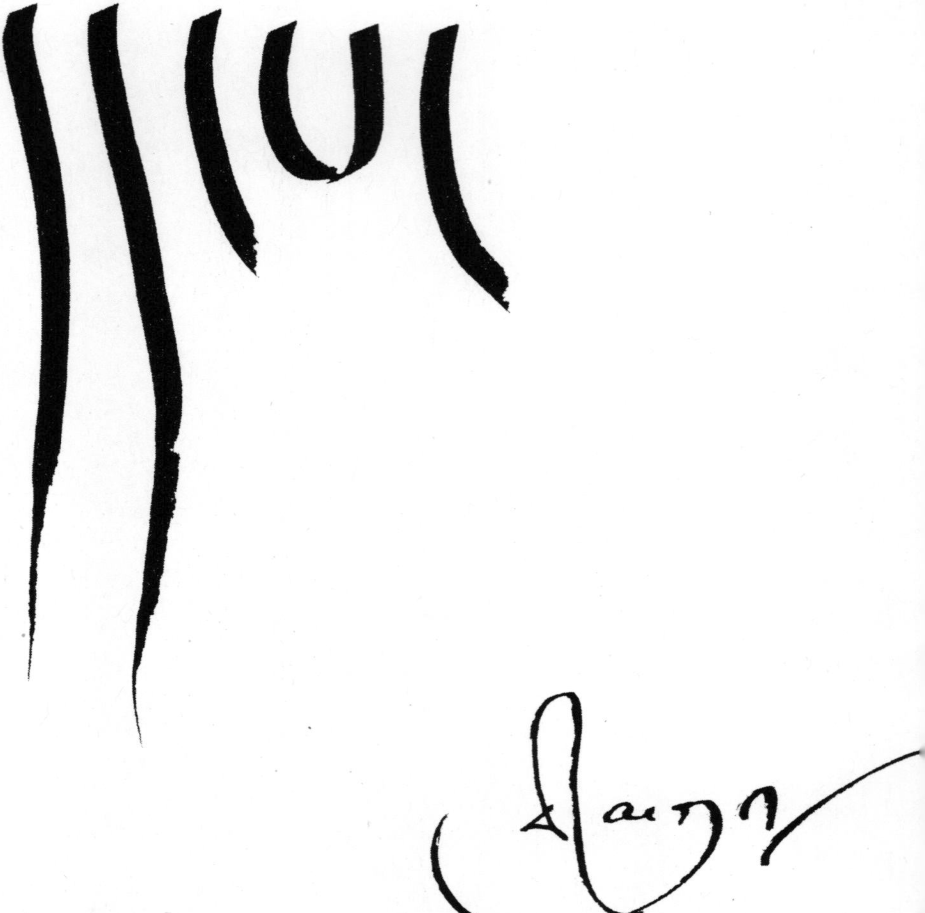

Working with a Spiritual Teacher

We need a good friend

Every human being wants to be happy and to enjoy happy circumstances. We all try to avoid painful and unpleasant things; no one wants pain and suffering. But, although our intentions are good, we usually don't know how to find true happiness and contentment. Most of the time we are running after things we think will make us happy, or running away from whatever makes us unhappy or gives us pain. But what we really lack is understanding and wisdom. That is why we need a spiritual friend or teacher who can give us positive guidance on how to rid ourselves of our unhappiness and how to become truly happy.

In Buddhism the spiritual teacher is generally called 'kalyanamitra'; that's the Sanskrit word. Kalyana means good deed or positive, so kalyana is something that brings well-being. Mitra means friend. Therefore, kalyanamitra means a friend that brings out positive things in you; someone who helps you to develop positive qualities and who will influences you in a positive way. In Tibetan it is translated as 'gewe shenyen'. Gewa means positive. Anything that results in well-being, happiness and joy is gewa.

Usually we are too engrossed in all our problems and much too busy in our daily lives, and we can easily lose sight of our positive aspirations.

So if we can find someone who can influence us in a good way, through their example, understanding and wisdom, this can exert such a good influence on us that we can become very inspired. It is said that the extent to which human beings can be influenced resembles a bow and arrow. Perhaps you have heard this before? I think it is a good analogy. When you draw a bow and arrow, the string touches the upper and lower parts of the bow but the longest part of the string is stretched and curved, not touching the bow. Following this analogy it can be said that there are some people who are not easily influenced, just as a small part of the string touches the top and bottom of the bow. But the vast majority of us are positioned somewhere within the curve of the bow string. It seems that very good people are not easily influenced but neither are very negative people. No matter what kind of friends they have or what kind of surroundings they live in, it is not possible for people at the top end to become negative. The same goes for the other end. Whatever positive influences come the way of very difficult and negative people, they are unable to change. But the rest of us, let's say 99.99 per cent, are more flexible and open and easily influenced. When we are in the company of positive and kind people we become better, and we tend to become worse in the company of negative people. These influences, good or bad, determine the way we behave most of the time.

The people we associate with, and especially the people we trust and learn from, and from whom we receive advice, must be trustworthy. They have to be experienced and wise, and also compassionate. From the Buddhist point of view, the spiritual friend, the teacher, is therefore very important. If you have a positive friend, you become positive. If you have a negative friend, then you can become negative also. That's why it's so very important.

Now this spiritual friend is sometimes called the guru. Guru means teacher actually. Guru in Sanskrit means nothing else but teacher. In Tibetan, the spiritual friend is also translated as lama and Kalu Rinpoche, a highly respected teacher, used to translate 'la' as high, or nothing above. And 'ma' means mother. So he said a Lama can be described as an excellent friend, like a mother. Someone who will nurture you and look after you. From this point of view, there is really no one more important or special than the lama.

So, in Buddhism, it is very important that we find a positive and genuine spiritual friend, teacher or guru. Also, it is as important to learn how to relate to the spiritual friend so that we can get the maximum benefit from the relationship. In all the different schools of Buddhism, and especially in Vajrayana, our development through the different stages of learning, understanding and meditation is very dependent on the teacher-student relationship. How much you understand and are able to bring of your own experience onto the path (whether you call that stages of enlightenment or just different stages of development, meditation and inner experience) depends on how much of an experienced friend or teacher you have. Otherwise it is very difficult to know how to proceed through the different stages.

When you have found a genuine spiritual friend or teacher it is considered a good beginning. 'Good beginning is half done.' This is because you have taken the first positive step and you have found your way onto the path. But it has to be emphasised that it is extremely important to find a genuine teacher, because if you follow the instructions of a false teacher you may take the wrong way and that can be extremely detrimental to you and your progress on the spiritual path. Therefore when you have found a real and genuine teacher it can be said that you have made a good beginning.

Examine the teacher

Finding the authentic teacher, the authentic spiritual friend, is the most important and basic thing from the Buddhist point of view, otherwise you could be completely misled and finding your way back can be very difficult. So in the Mahayana, and in every Vajrayana text, the first topic always discussed is how to examine the spiritual friend. You have to examine whether the teacher, spiritual friend, or the lama you follow is a genuinely good one or not. You cannot just follow anybody.

But how do we do that? What is the best way of doing this? How do we examine the teacher? First, we take into consideration the most important thing, the teachings. How much we can trust the teacher depends on his or her teachings. So we have to examine his or her teachings and reflect on them. That's the first thing. And then, according to our own understanding and knowledge of the Dharma, of the tradition and scriptures, we can decide whether that person is teaching according to the teachings of the Buddha or not. So, we need to know whether a particular teacher has received enough education and training and whether he or she has any real experience of the teachings or not. It is not the personality of the teacher that is of prime importance, but the teachings. It is the practice, the path we want to follow. That's the most important thing for us. Therefore we rely primarily on the instructions, the teachings given to us by our spiritual friend.

The teachings we receive must be based on a line of experienced masters and realised teachers, they must come from a genuine tradition. If the tradition you follow is not a genuine one, then you will not receive the right teachings. In addition, we must be able to understand and make use of the teachings we receive, based on our own logic, reason and experience. The teachings must be something we reasonably understand and can put into practice. That is the path.

So first we examine the knowledge, understanding, and experience of the teacher, and then we examine their compassion. That is regarded as very important because, if your spiritual friend has no compassion, they might not want to truly help and in fact cannot really help you due to their lack of compassion. They might be trying to benefit themselves rather than you, and also they may be trying to exploit you. From the

Buddhist point of view, whether someone has attained any realisation or not is judged by how compassionate they are.

So, you have to ascertain if the person you are going to take on as your teacher has compassion or not. This is one of the most important elements in judging whether a particular teacher is a reliable one, a genuine one or not. Because when somebody is really compassionate, even if he does not know exactly how to answer a question, he would never mislead you, or try to put you down by pointing out your faults to others. On the other hand, if he is not compassionate, even if he has an extensive knowledge of the teachings, he might not tell you anything because of his lack of good intentions and compassion. When the teacher's motivation is wrong, everything else will be wrong too.

After that, the most important thing is a willingness to share, a willingness to help and teach. These three qualities are essential and must be taken into consideration when looking for a teacher. The first is that the teacher you choose has understanding, experience and knowledge; the second is that he or she must be compassionate, and the third that he or she must be willing to teach.

The most special relationship

Now, having found such a spiritual friend, how do you relate to the teacher? In our Kagyu tradition we read the stories of Milarepa, Naropa and many others. In the case of Milarepa it is said that as soon as he heard the name of Marpa his teacher, the hairs on his body stood up and his eyes welled up with tears. He had absolutely no doubt from that moment on and said, "I must go to this man. He is my guru and I will follow him no matter what happens." Even when he was told by Marpa to build a house and dismantle it single-handedly four times, he had no doubts.

Naropa was a great master, one of the most learned Buddhists at that time. He was a professor at Nalanda University. He was sitting there one day reading a very complicated tantric text and he was thinking to himself: "People say I am very learned, and I am really very learned because I understand everything." He was very happy with himself and rather proud! He thought he understood everything. After a short while, a shadow fell on his book, he looked up and there was this very old woman standing beside him, looking down at him. Her eyes seemed to pierce through him as she said: "You don't know a thing, you know absolutely nothing!" Naropa looked up and exclaimed: "That's right! I don't know anything. I only know the words. I don't know what all of this means from my experience. I don't really know anything." So then he asked: "Who does know, then?" And she replied "Tilopa, my brother, he knows."

And immediately, as in Milarepa's case, Naropa had no doubts. "Yes, I must find Tilopa." He didn't even bother to put his books away, he just stood up and left and didn't return for thirteen years. Eventually he found Tilopa, but Tilopa gave him no end of trouble. He gave Naropa many crazy tasks to do, some really impossible things. It is said that Naropa almost died thirteen times trying to please Tilopa. But these are rare stories about very special people; extraordinary teachings and achievements, devotion and doubtlessness. We cannot say that all of us will have to go through such things. Most likely we won't.

I have met people who say "I have been waiting for my guru to appear for 15 years, when is he going to come? What shall I do in the meantime?" They become completely frustrated. He may or may not come. We must not wait until it happens. There is no need to become frustrated. Finding the teachings and the instructions are the most important things. This enables us to take the first step, to begin to learn. It doesn't matter so much from whom we receive the teachings. We learn and practise them for a while and when we have some insight into the teachings, and some experience of them, our trust in the teacher will grow naturally. So the more we know the teacher or the spiritual friend, the more our confidence grows. This confidence and trusting faith is not something that happens immediately, although this might be the case for some people. But usually it has to develop slowly. It's based on understanding, based on experience. So you don't just look at him or her and say: "Wow, I trust this person completely." Usually it does not happen like that. I have to understand the teacher and get to know him or her better. After some time the trust will develop. And the more my understanding of the teachings develops, the greater the trust will grow.

This is a relationship based on understanding and teaching. It's not just another personal relationship. The more we experience and understand the teachings, the more our trust and faith in the teacher develops and the more our devotion grows. I just talked about Milarepa. Milarepa's best student was Gampopa and he also had a strong and close relationship with his teacher. Milarepa had given Gampopa all the teachings and instructions, and Gampopa had practised them intensively. When Gampopa finished his training, Milarepa said: "Now you can go, now you can go home" - Gampopa's home was in central Tibet - "You go back home and practise there. One day you will see me, your old father, as the real Buddha, and that will be the time when you can teach others." By this Milarepa meant that when you can see your teacher as the real Buddha, this means that you have the full realisation of what the teacher has taught you.

But, who is the real Buddha? Buddha is the one who shows you the way, the one who helps you understand the path. Buddha is no one else. The actual activity of the Buddha is to give the teachings and to guide and show the way. If the teacher has shown you the way and you have experienced it in yourself, then you will feel such gratitude and faith, such understanding and devotion arising in you that you will see that person as a complete Buddha. The more trust you are able to generate, the more devotion you will develop for your teacher and this means the teachings have helped you. This means you have understood, and that is a direct consequence of your devotion.

What I want to make clear is that trust and faith in the teacher has to be developed through personal experience of the teachings and the practice. It is not possible to experience that kind of absolute devotion and complete trust right from the beginning. For common beings, as we are, who might not have complete trust in our spiritual friend from the beginning, then that is okay; it's fine. We can't do anything else at that point. But it is necessary to continue to examine the teacher. The more we examine and find his or her good qualities, the more we are likely to trust, and the more open we will be to the teachings and our understanding of them will grow. And also, the more open we become, the more we benefit from the teachings. This is something that has to be understood clearly. Firstly we find a positive teacher, and work with that. Also, we continue to examine the teacher and the teachings. Slowly, as we understand more, trust will grow and blossom into devotion.

But it is very important that all this is based on the teachings. The Buddha said, "Don't rely on the personality of the teacher; rely on the Dharma." So it's not that the teacher is more important than the Dharma. The Dharma is more important than the teacher. But when you rely on the Dharma, and understand it, your confidence will grow and your trust in the person who teaches you will also grow. If you can see that your teacher acts according to the Dharma, then you will naturally have trust in your teacher because you trust the Dharma.

Devotion

Guru yoga practice is a practice where we use the guru as a meditation technique, as a practice, to bring out in our meditation the essential nature of our own mind. We do this in order to bring out our Buddha nature so that we can become completely open and natural. During this practice we use devotion as a medium because trust and devotion are very important practice mediums. And devotion is a very clear emotion. Through trust and devotion we can open our hearts and opening our hearts is the main practice. Devotion is a positive emotion. It is not a concept. It is clear, it is bright and a very strong medium in meditation.

And Guru yoga is the best way to generate devotion. It's not just because Guru yoga is based on your own spiritual friend or teacher but also because it brings with it the energy of all the past enlightened beings. We use the enlightened energy of all the Buddhas and Bodhisattvas and, of course, of your own teacher.

Your teacher is chosen by you, it is not the other way around. That is very important to remember. The student finds the teacher. From all the different traditions and schools, and from all the great and kind masters and teachers, we select our teacher using our own judgement. We chose the teacher we feel we can trust and who will help us the most. So, from all the people I have met or known, this is the one with whom I feel the strongest connection, and I am able to trust this teacher and his teachings and everything else about him or her. I can put all my trust in him or her. And through this medium I can develop even more trust and devotion. Guru yoga is used in this way to bring out our own openness and trust. That's the practice, and within that practice you try to see everything as positive and as the display of the teacher.

The guru, from the Buddhist point of view, is not just a person. The guru is not only the outer teacher, but also the inner teacher. This is so important because it's actually the inner teacher that decides on the outer teacher. The inner teacher is our own basic goodness; our own Buddha nature, our own primordial wisdom. And within this process everything becomes our teacher, this is called 'the guru of the signs.' Every appearance, everything around us can be the teacher. We can learn from every arising. That is the main practice. Therefore, through the guidance of the outer teacher, we are able to come into contact with our inner teacher, and through that interaction, we can learn from everything that appears, so that absolutely everything becomes our teacher. That is the proper way to relate to the teacher.

Rely on the Dharma

The most important thing in the teacher-student relationship is to learn the Dharma. It's very important to ask questions and to communicate, otherwise nothing much happens. Milarepa said of Gampopa: "He is the one who has learned the fastest. He is my lineage holder, because he knows how to ask questions." Learning is vital. It's not enough to say: "This is my lama." You need to receive teachings, and he needs to answer your questions, and also to explain again and again whatever you have not completely understood. In that way your own understanding is clarified and you can make progress.

As I said earlier, there is no need to rely on personalities, rely on the Dharma. And you do not have to rely on the guru for everything. You must have freedom. It is a misconception that you hand over your freedom to your guru. That's wrong. Your life is your life; it doesn't belong to your guru or anyone else. Of course you can learn from the guru as to what would be the best thing to do, or not to do, in a particular situation but nobody can take over you or your life. If you ask your teacher: "Should I have my breakfast at eight or nine o'clock?" then he might answer: "Why not?" or "Maybe, maybe not, when you have the time." When you ask the teacher a question he has to give you an answer. If you ask him what colour toilet paper you should use, he might say it doesn't matter, or that he prefers white! But really these questions are unnecessary, we can all see that. The main thing is the practice and the help the teacher can give you to guide you on the path of Dharma. Of course there is nothing wrong in asking your teacher about a certain situation in your life, but sometimes this can cause problems for the student and the teacher. It happens sometimes that some students misunderstand when the teacher gives advice, and they say that their teacher always tells them what to do, or not do. But the whole process of the teacher-student relationship is to learn how to free ourselves from fear and aversion. It is about liberation. That is the correct understanding.

You have to learn for yourself how to become free; how to be free in your mind. You have to learn how to be courageous so that you can make the right decisions in your life. This is what you learn from the guru.

In the teacher-student relationship the most important thing is learning the Dharma and the best way to practice it. But learning in this sense is not just about receiving information. Learning here is about the direct experience of the Dharma, the path. This experience is not something that can be given to you by another. It is your personal experience of the Path. Your practice has to go deeper and deeper in your understanding and then your actions should be in accordance with that. Also, it is not necessary to receive many practices. After you have gone deeply into one practice and you feel you understand it, whatever experiences come up, you then talk to your teacher about them. You try to explain your experiences in order to clarify them and go forward. And in the process, the path becomes an exchange of experiences between you and your teacher. The experience of learning from your teacher is not like going to a university lecture when you listen to the lecturer, and take notes, and that's that - finished! It is more experiential, more practical. You go through a deeper understanding of the different levels of experience. It is a ripening process that takes time and practice. It does not happen easily or effortlessly.

Communication between teacher and student can be difficult sometimes. I might have something in my mind I want to say, and your mind might be hearing something completely different when I say it.

So sometimes it's very difficult for you to understand exactly what I'm saying. It happens many times that, although we are both using the same words, communication does not go well. The same words have different meanings for different people. It is said that, as a rule, every talk has four different versions. The first version is the one the speaker wants to convey, then the second is the version that he actually gives. The third version is the one that people hear (actually that could be many versions) and then there is the version that is reported! One talk, four different versions. Communicating is not easy because I cannot experience you, and how you are and feel directly. And you cannot experience me. So, to try to pass on someone's experience to another is very difficult. A lot of effort goes into that. But there has to be trust and it has to be a meaningful exchange. The stronger the trust, the better it will be. As I mentioned before, we cannot have that kind of trust from the very beginning. That is usually not possible.

Questions & Answers

Student: You said it's the Dharma that's important, that we should not be drawn to the personalities. But might it not be easier, at the commencement of this student-teacher relationship, to feel some empathy with the personality of the teacher?

Rinpoche: It might happen like that. Sometimes it happens when you meet a great teacher, a great master. I know many people who met the 16th Karmapa, and they all say, "I didn't know anything about anything but I just cannot imagine not trusting this person completely." Also in the case of the Dalai Lama many people just see him once, and they know that they can trust him completely. So many people become interested in the Dharma just through meeting great masters. But the most important thing is still the teachings. Because it is entirely possible that you meet His Holiness the Dalai Lama, and genuine devotion arises in you, and that's good. But later, it might happen that somebody says something that creates a doubt in your mind, and you may say to yourself, "Maybe I was wrong". That kind of initial undiluted trust can easily come to an end when doubt arises. When you understand the teachings in a deeper way, it is more difficult to entertain such doubts. That's why the actual experience that your practice brings is so important.

Student: I was wondering, Rinpoche, you mentioned devotion as being a clear emotion. Could you say something more about what you mean by a clear emotion?

Rinpoche: Clear emotion means an opening of the heart. When devotion arises it opens the heart, and at the same time something happens to your body. It is inspiring. It is not interrupted by thoughts and ideas. It is an emotion and it arises like any other emotion. Devotion comes straight from the heart.

Student: Spacious?

Rinpoche: Spacious, maybe. But that is not what I meant by clear. What I mean by clear is that devotion is not a confused emotion. It's the heart opening, it is inspiring. When devotion arises something happens in your heart. Your hair may stand on end and your eyes well up with tears, yet thoughts do not arise at that moment. Your mind becomes very clear and thoughts, confusion and doubts do not arise. There is only this clear emotion. I think people understand this. No?

Student: If one's teacher isn't around physically that often, is Guru yoga the best thing to do, to practise, to keep that devotion alive?

Rinpoche: In the Guru yoga practice it doesn't matter if your teacher is near or far. It is a strong practice. Actually, sometimes I think it really hasn't much to do with the actual guru! But, you need to learn and communicate with your teacher. There is a saying: "Your guru neither too far nor too near, that is best." Because if he is too far then you can never meet him, and that's not good. And if he is too near, you see too many problems. That's also not too good! So you meet sometimes, and it's okay. You use that time to clarify your problems, whether you understood the teachings correctly or not. The main thing is to clarify your practice and to receive as many teachings as possible. But you don't need to receive all the teachings from just one guru. And I believe that it's not even necessary to have just one guru. Other people seem to think the same. It's not like marriage, you know! You can have many gurus. There is no problem with that. I don't have any problems with that.

Student: Rinpoche, I was very struck by what you were saying about the inner guru, and it made me think about something I certainly have experienced. I know other people have told me they have also experienced a similar thing. When you are going through very difficult times, you have a kind of a friendly voice inside, not a different voice from your own. You connect with something in you that feels very wise and compassionate. It is something in yourself, not necessarily connected with anybody else you know. And I wondered whether that's the kind of experience of the inner guru?

Rinpoche: Maybe you can call that the inner guru. An inner intuition. Maybe I shouldn't say too much about that. We need to also listen to our inner voice, but that can be a little tricky sometimes. It could be your ego speaking, trying to justify something we have done or are about to do, and then saying it is the guru speaking. Therefore listen to your inner voice, but not too much.

Student: Please could you say something about your gurus, your own masters.

Rinpoche: I have too many gurus! I consider my main teachers as His Holiness the 16th Karmapa, and Dilgo Khyentse Rinpoche. And then I have many, many lamas with whom I have studied, and I consider all of them my gurus. And I really think that some of them were realised, and extremely compassionate.

Student: Rinpoche, what about outer guru devotion? You don't seem to encourage prostrations. You seem to be more informal. How do you feel about people showing outer forms of respect, like prostrations?

Rinpoche: Prostrating to the teacher is a tradition. Respecting the teacher is respecting the teachings. In Indian society and in Tibetan society, they put the teacher on a high throne, show lots of respect and then make prostrations which are not necessarily showing respect to the person, but to the teachings. It is a way of showing how much you value the instructions and teachings. That's the way it is. If you make prostrations as a sense of showing respect and also in order to subdue your own pride, then that is okay. But this is sometimes misunderstood. It might be seen as a part of Tibetan theocracy: the lamas sit on high thrones and you all have to prostrate to them! And if you see it that way, then it's not helpful.

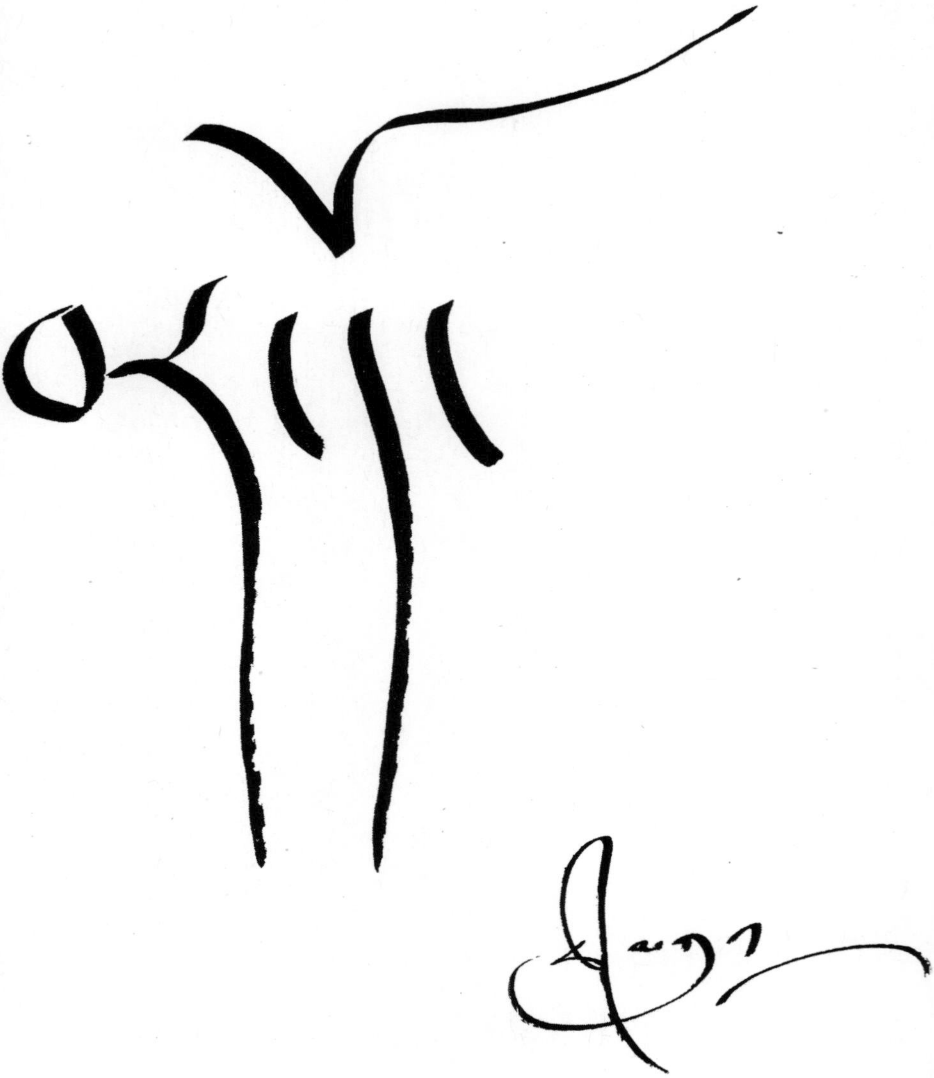

Death & Dying

That which we fear most

It sometimes seems to me that death is a word we don't want to mention and people try to avoid even thinking about it. But it is part of life; as soon as we are born we start to die. Someone sent me recently a You Tube video where a baby is born and it shoots from its mother like a rocket! It was actually very funny. As it is crying (it sounds like one continuous terrifying "arghhhhhhhhhh!") the baby flies through the air and it grows older and older, first growing into a bigger child, then a young man, and finally an old man. The film finishes with the old man crashing into his grave. Perhaps it is not quite like that for us, we usually have some life in between. But most of us are afraid of death, it is the unknown. Actually there is no one who doesn't fear death. Especially those who boast that they don't, they usually fear it all the more.

From a Buddhist point of view, most of our fears in life are related to death and also to birth. Birth and death are regarded as the two main sources of our traumatic mind. Of course there are others, but our basic and deepest level of trauma comes from these two. So it's not useful to try to ignore death, because it cannot be ignored. Not only is it certain that we will die, but our loved ones will also die. We all have lost people we have loved very much and it is very important to face that, because the only way to deal with and overcome our fears is to face them. By facing that which we fear most and trying to understand it clearly, we can see the true nature of our fear. So it is important that we understand deeply what death is, and also face the inevitability of death, in order to really prepare for it. Death is something that is studied deeply in all the Buddhist traditions. It is researched in different ways, talked about, reflected upon and used in our daily practice too.

Everything changes

The most important fact to reflect upon is that our life changes. This change is a natural thing, in the sense that there's something changing all the time. But we often wish that everything should remain the same, unchanged. When you ask little children what they are going to be when they grow up, they usually say: "I'm going to stay like this." We would like things to remain as they are; but that is never possible. We can't remain children forever.

Sometimes people celebrate their birthdays and sometimes they don't. Some people don't want to celebrate because it is too much for them to bear; they seem almost traumatised by it. Yesterday I was 59 and today I'm 60! But we have to remember that we don't only change on our birthdays, we are always changing. Change is the natural way of all life. In a way, every moment is a death and a birth, every day is a death and birth because we go to sleep at night and then we get up in the morning. I was told by somebody that at the end of the day our body has become smaller by a few millimetres. I don't know by how many exactly, but then the next morning we are back to our normal height. We are constantly changing. But, of course, death is a very big change because we leave our body behind and the body dissolves into the four elements. And when we look at our consciousness, we see that it has its own continuum. This is the main understanding from a Buddhist point of view.

Awareness

When we are alive, body and mind are almost inseparable, they are interdependent. Whatever happens in our mind also reflects in our body and whatever happens in our body also reflects in our mind. Some people believe that they experience things in either a psychological or a physical way and they feel the physical experience is something much stronger than the psychological one. But anything that you experience with the mind is also physical because it will be experienced by the body too.

When we feel sadness or any other emotion, it immediately shows in a physical way. You see it on your face; you feel it in your body. Fear is physical and so is pain. When I feel angry my face becomes red and blue, my eyes bulge out, and there is almost smoke coming out of my ears! Not quite but almost. All this is physical. Mind and body influence each other, they experience things together.

But, more than this, the Buddhist understanding is that the mind has the characteristic of being aware and this awareness is not only restricted to the body. The mind can be aware of much more than our body and what is within it. We can see and experience beyond the time and space we are in. Therefore, the mind has its own continuum.

This aspect of the mind has been experienced by many meditators and different kinds of psychic people. Also by people who have gone through the near death experience. Even when you are not physically able to have contact with anybody, even when you are declared dead, your mind is able to see what is happening around you, as well as beyond your normal view. So from this point of view, the mind is not just the body. It has its own continuum, just as the body also has its own continuum. It is very important to consider this. If the body is just the same as the mind, and the mind is only part of the body, then when the body dies there would be nothing to fear because that would be the end of everything. On the other hand, if there is a continuum, what is it that continues, and how? Well, this is very important from the Buddhist point of view. Awareness itself continues. Awareness is not a thing; it's not something you can put in a box or something you can catch hold of in a pincer and say, "this is it." Therefore, since awareness has no physical substance it cannot be extinguished or destroyed; it must continue, it must go on. Also, we have to remember that there is no need to be afraid because death is just one more change in this continuum. A greater change maybe than sleep and waking up but just another change. It is not the end. This is the understanding of many spiritual traditions. But from the Buddhist view, death is not only a continuation, death is an opportunity.

Everything changes every moment. Life is a constant change. The death process is also a constant change; we call it the bardo, which means in-between, or transition. Life is a transition just as death is a transition; it is all a cycle of transition, a kind of journey. Therefore we have this great opportunity when we are alive, when we have attained this wonderful human life, to take this as our journey, our path. We need to remember how fortunate we are to have this precious human life because it's very important to acknowledge and accept the positive side of our life.

Happiness

We may have many problems in our life; there are many problems everywhere in the world but still we have life. We have so many good things that we can enjoy and do in our life. But, from the Buddhist point of view, this life is important because it offers us the opportunity to find true peace, joy and happiness. Whether I am happy or not, whether my mind is joyful and peaceful, satisfied or not, does not depend on what I have or what is going on around me. It depends on how I experience myself. If we can really learn how to experience ourselves in a proper way, in a deep way, how to bring out our natural peace and happiness in a profound way, we can be the happiest person on earth, and that is a great opportunity.

I was talking recently to a scientist who was telling me about research into the effects of meditation. They conducted a test on the brain of a certain Lama who had been meditating for many years. They already knew that there is a certain part of the brain that registers how happy a person is and they wanted to see if this part is changed in someone who meditates. They found that in this person's brain that area was a thousand times more active than in the average person's brain. So their immediate reaction was that something must be wrong with the equipment they were using to measure the brain activity. They thought the test must have been wrong somehow. So they carried out more tests in different parts of the world, on different equipment, on the same Lama. But they found exactly the same results. And they said this is impossible, it cannot be, so they kept these results secret. Either this man is totally mad or there is something wrong with the test, they thought. But then they did the test on others, other Lamas who had also done long-term meditation, and they found similar results. Therefore it appears that there is a way to attain this happiness through meditation. If you really practice, you can be happy!

Death, the greatest opportunity

We have this opportunity to attain happiness and liberation in this very life but also much more so at the time of death. Because at the time of death, when our outer body and what we call the gross mind (or more solid mental factors) dissolve, our emotions manifest and dissolve in this deep level of consciousness which is the most natural state of mind. It is uncontaminated by concepts and emotions and it is something we can all experience. When the natural state of mind is experienced and it is recognised, it is possible for us to liberate ourselves from our problems, emotions and reactions. In this state, our usual way of reacting emotionally, our habitual way of rejection and other negative emotions is unnecessary. So it is said that we can be free within that state. What continues is the most enlightened, the most realised, the deepest level of peace, joyfulness and compassion.

Death is similar to the sleeping state. When we go to sleep our consciousness goes deeper and deeper. It goes so deep that we become unconscious. From this state we come up to a lighter kind of sleep, then we dream and slowly we wake up. Death is a similar process. We go into what we call the clear light. This is the deepest level of our consciousness. It is a very subtle level of consciousness, untainted by emotions. Here we can experience enlightenment. But if we are unable to recognise it we come up again into a consciousness that is similar to the dream state. Basically, this bardo state is like the dream state. It is similar to when we are dreaming but think we are awake. It is as if we have a dream body where we have all sorts of different experiences and everything is very clear but we don't have a physical body. The bardo state is said to be like that.

When we dream we are conscious but the way we react at the dream level is not actually the way we react when we are awake. In the dream state we are more driven by our subconscious and our habitual tendencies. So therefore, it is always said that the way we experience our dreams, the way we react in them is similar to the way we will react in the bardo after death. We have dream yoga exercises in Buddhism, where we try to train in our dreams. If we can do this well, if we react in a more positive way in our dreams, it is a good preparation for our own death. Then, when we find ourselves in the bardo we will understand clearly and recognise that the bardo state is very much like a dream. We will then go through it as we go through a dream, nothing more and nothing less.

Because when we realise a dream is only a dream, we react differently than when we didn't know it is a dream.

Once I dreamt I was eaten and swallowed by a tiger. I was telling myself, "Now I am in the belly of the tiger" and was wondering what it would be like inside its belly. When I realised it was a dream there was no problem and no fear. This kind of realisation does not happen to me very often but sometimes it does. If you are really able to train while in your dreams, and you wish to make something happen to yourself or your circumstances, you can make it happen because it is a dream.

This level of understanding is what we also need in the bardo. In the bardo we only have a mental body, like in a dream. So, for example, if you want to be somewhere, go anywhere immediately, your mind can make it happen. You are suddenly there! It can happen because in the bardo there is nothing but mind.

The real practice: being with what is

This kind of understanding and way of experiencing right now, whether through meditation, reflection or mind training exercises, is a preparation for dying. It's not just saying that I won't be afraid at the time of dying, but it's with the understanding that there is no need for fear, because that fear doesn't prevent anything negative from happening. I can fear my head off but it doesn't stop anything! Only more trouble and fear arises. Fear is completely useless; it does not help in the least. It is very important to understand that with the help of training and meditation, and through my own understanding, I am able to let these experiences come and go, whether they are positive or negative. Any experience is in fact nothing more than an arising in my own awareness. I cannot experience anything other than myself, my own experiences. It is a manifestation or display of my own mind because there is no experience outside my mind. So when I experience something nice - it's nice- but that is also my mind experiencing that. It arises or comes out of my mind and when it goes, it just dissolves into my mind. There's nowhere else for it to go.

All experiences are reflections, manifestations of my mind. So nice thoughts and emotions, pleasant experiences and sensations, arise and dissolve within my mind. They are like the waves of the ocean, like the sun and its rays, like my body and its shadow. It is all my own. When I can see and understand that deeply, whether there is sadness or joy arising in my mind I can let it be, I can relax in that. Now there is sadness arising in my mind, I can let it be and I can relax in that. Now joy arises in my mind, enjoy it in a relaxed way. Good things come and go and also bad things. Everything changes. It doesn't matter much. This is the natural flow of things, everything comes and goes. It is almost like bubbles in water. You should not grasp too strongly, nor react with strong aversion and say this is, or is not, a nice thing. Sometimes when there is too much of a nice thing, it is no longer that nice. When you know how to let things come and go, you can find that anything can be okay. You can take everything in your stride. Then you can understand and learn to live your life and how to be content at any time. When that is understood and experienced deeply, you learn that dying is also okay. Whatever happens, living or dying, you are alright with everything. When that understanding happens, we have become stable, our mind has become stable. It doesn't matter what happens, we are not shaken by things. That experience is the true preparation for death, and also for life.

Helping ourselves and others

So, with the understanding that life and death are not two different things, but two sides of the same coin, and that this is a continuous and interdependent process, a transition; we have less worry and fear. The more stable we become, the more deeply we can learn to just be. Then it is also possible to help others. Because unless I am stable myself, I cannot help others. Therefore to help myself, to work on myself, is the first and most important thing. And when even just a little bit of that stability happens, a little bit of confidence also happens, and then more compassion arises. I don't always have to run after or away from things because I find that I am fine with whatever happens. Our usual reaction is to run from or towards something. All stress and worries come as a result of that. We become stressed trying to fix things, to manipulate things, to run away from things, and that makes us very unhappy. But, with a bit of understanding, we can begin to change the way we see and react to things. When I become more peaceful, I am also able to be kinder and more compassionate. I can give more, be more generous to people. I can be more loving and I can share more. I can even help at many different levels. The most important thing people need, whether they are living or dying is love. We all need love and people who will care for us. That is what friendship means. I need to feel that I am important to somebody. Someone cares about me and I matter to them. There isn't a person in the world that does not need to be loved and cared for. So, if we are stable and peaceful, we can be more understanding with those who are experiencing a lot of fear, whether in life or dying, and we can tell them that there is no need to be so anxious and afraid. It is possible to go through these things without having too much anxiety, panic and fear.

The main understanding is to try to help ourselves and others, through good times and difficult times. I think it's very important to be very aware of how things can change so quickly, it's very important to be aware of impermanence. When people hear the word impermanence they can sometimes feel very afraid. But talking about impermanence, change and dying, is a very useful thing too. I read a story somewhere that there was a person in prison, and on the prison wall someone had written, 'This Will Also Pass.' He came out of prison after many years and he said that those words saved his life. Every morning and every evening he read them and that gave him the courage to survive his sentence because he knew that it would also pass, that it was impermanent.

So from that point of view everything will pass, and then you can see that it's not a bad thing that things change and that's the natural way of everything. It is not something morbid and dreadful. Good things come and go, not so good things will come and go, and bad things also come and go. It is up to you how bad or good you make it. You can react to things with a positive state of mind, because any bad thing has also a good side.

When His Holiness the Dalai Lama is asked about the situation in Tibet he always says that it is true that this is the worst period in our history. But, he also says that if we only focus on the negative side of events and just complain that the Chinese are terrible and nobody comes to our help, then our spirits will sink lower and lower and we would become really depressed. We would become so despondent that everything would be meaningless. This doesn't do anybody any good. Therefore, we must think very clearly and realise that we are in a very difficult situation; but we cannot just stay there. We must think about what can be done so that the situation improves in some way, otherwise we can end up in a worse situation. Actually, this is a very easy thing to do because when you are really low anything is an improvement. So we all should concentrate on that, improving the situation we are in. We can always find something to make things better and when we do that we also feel better, because we are more optimistic about the outcome. When we approach things that way even the worst situation can be improved.

When we focus only on negative things everything becomes problematic. But if we are able to widen our perspective and focus on something positive, something good we can do to change our situation, the whole atmosphere of our experience changes.

Questions & Answers

Student: Rinpoche, it was quite refreshing to hear your last words when you conveyed an optimistic view to try to always see something better out of a bad situation. Because in the west, the answer we give to children is very often, 'Well, it could be far worse.'

Rinpoche: But that's not too bad either, because that means it's not the worst.

Student: Rinpoche, the awareness that we have when we are alive, is that the same after death? Would we recognise it? I think what I'm saying is that if I'm scared at the moment of death, my mind will become very neurotic and clinging, and any awareness that I have attained while being alive might turn into its opposite.

Rinpoche: The understanding is that how we are now, my state of mind at this moment is the result of my past. That means that whatever happened in my past, all the things that have made me what I am now, and the way I react to them, is as a result of the things that have happened to me in the past. So therefore, how you are in the dying process or after death, is also the product of all the past experiences you bring with you. The idea is that if we are generally more peaceful and more together in the difficult times we experience in this life now, in our day-to-day life, you would react like that at the time of death also. That's the general understanding. That's why they say to look at your dreams. How you react to bad dreams and nightmares is said to be a kind of test. How you react in your dreams will be how you will react at the time of your death.

Student: I've done a lot of spiritual practice in my life and I have a background of that kind of thing. But lately I've been in situations that have been really 'pushing my buttons' as they say. What I've been finding is that after a while I react in an extremely habitual way, and then afterwards I tend to withdraw from the situation so I can calm down a bit. It doesn't take long to get back to a state of understanding when it's not so bad. Then I go back to the on-going situation. I'm okay for a bit and then suddenly sort of 'ping!' it comes back. Is it better to avoid the situations that provoke you or is it better to face these challenges? Is it a kind of practice like working a muscle? Sometimes I think I should maybe run away and not put myself under so much pressure but this makes me feel I am avoiding practice. Other times I feel it's good for me because at least there is some movement.

Rinpoche: Life is what it is, no? I mean it's not as if I don't want anything problematic or negative or provocative happening and I can just push it away, or run away and I will not have problems. Problems are bound to come. But when there are no problems I don't think you should or need to be looking for them. But when they come you have to face them. You have to learn how to deal with them. Of course, all your emotions will be there and all your negative habitual tendencies will come up. But I think if you manage to go through these difficult situations without too much damage, then it shows you have achieved something from your practice. I am sure that you have to congratulate yourself for that.

Student: Rinpoche, I wondered what advice you had for people who are with someone who is dying. Quite a while ago I was with someone who was dying and although I was kind to them and listened to them I did feel a little bit useless. I didn't really know how to help them or if it was even possible to really help them, and wondered what was really possible for me to do in those circumstances?

Rinpoche: It is a very difficult time when people are dying. How much you can help depends on many things, sometimes I'm sure there's nothing much you can do. The dying person is going through all these other experiences I have talked about. These cannot be shared. So we cannot help the dying person that much. When I'm dying it is something that only I can go through and I cannot share it, even with my dearest and nearest friend, so they cannot really do much. The only thing you can do is give him or her loving care and maybe help them understand a little that there is no need to be so afraid. I have seen this happening, that when people understand, even a little, that fear is useless, they become less fearful of dying. This can make a real difference but it is not just a question of telling them this. It is something very difficult and personal.

Student: How do Buddhists understand or translate the definitions of hell and paradise in Christianity?

Rinpoche: Buddhists also have the concepts of paradise and hell, although the Buddhist concepts of hell and paradise are also impermanent. Even if you go to hell, it's not forever and neither is paradise. Paradise and hell are said to be states of mind. If your emotional and mental state of mind and your way of reacting is very negative, then you have an experience of hell; and if it is a more positive state of mind, then you have an experience of paradise. So with this in mind, it is easy to create a hell or a heaven for yourself, and when you are in these states of mind, they become very real to you. That's the main understanding. It feels very real, although it is more or less a state of mind.

Student: Rinpoche, I agreed for a long time and still agree with this, that this transition, death, doesn't really matter, but once you have children things change a bit. Thank god I've never experienced this; so far all the deaths I have experienced in my life have been quite joyful. Whoever died around me, I was there and it was fine. But I really don't want to experience the death of my children or myself dying while they are young. The game has changed for me, there's a difference in the quality of death.

Rinpoche: It is true that the most painful thing that can happen to parents is to see the death of their children. To see the death of any young person is very painful. Dying when they are still young means they have not experienced life fully. It is not only painful for the parents, but for everybody else too. Of course, death is very painful for everybody, no matter who they are. Your loved ones have gone and this is not something you can ever forget. So it is not a nice thing to experience. And yet, it is also a fact that everything changes and whether you like it or not life is uncertain. Even if you are healthy there's no guarantee you will not die. When you are old there is no guarantee you will die soon either. If you are sick it is also not guaranteed you will die. Sometimes, as the saying goes, during the lifetime of a terminally ill person hundreds and thousands of totally fit and healthy people die. That's a fact. Some die in the mother's womb, some people die after they are born, others die when they are a little baby or at a young age; some people die when they are young men or women, and some people die when they are very old. Therefore this is something we have to understand deeply. I think the most important thing is to learn to live in the most loving and harmonious way in the little time we have when we are together. Time goes by really fast and even a hundred years is a short time. Twenty, thirty years can go just like that, in the blink of an eye. We don't notice how quickly time passes. Many years ago, I went to one of my colleague's wedding celebrations, and after a while I had this idea in my head that the marriage had happened about three years ago. One day a bearded man came to one of my talks and he said to me, "My father sent me to say hello to you." "Who is your father?" I asked. He gave the name of his father and I realised his father was my friend whose wedding I attended just as if it was yesterday! Life is very short, so the little time we have with our friends, with our family, parents, and children we should live as happily and as lovingly as we can. I don't think there is any time to spend fighting. I think this attitude is very important.

There is a story, I think from the Jataka stories, the Buddha's tales. There once was a family, an old mother and father and they had a young son who was married and had a child. They were so loving and good towards each other that they became an example for the whole area. Then suddenly one day the son died, the young son. All the villagers were devastated and very sad; they went to the family to give their condolences. But neither the father nor the mother seemed to be very sad. The man's wife was doing her usual things and seemed to be doing them quite happily. So the villagers asked if it was true that their son had died and the family confirmed it was true. The villagers couldn't understand why they were not sad or in mourning. The father of the family said: "Life is like that. We were together as a family but we knew that any one of us could die at any moment. That's the way life is. Because we knew this, we all decided to love each other as much as we could. We tried to live each day in the most loving and kindest way, because we all knew that any one of us could die at any minute and then it would be too late to grieve. We never knew who would die the earliest, but every day we tried to live happily and we loved each other the most we could. So now that it has happened we are happy that we took that action and that we lived so happily together. We have no regrets and there is no need of mourning."

Of course it is very good that we do everything to avert death if we can, especially the death of the young ones. Nevertheless, I think sometimes it's good to remind ourselves that anything can happen at any time and that we need to be prepared for that. This preparation should make us closer to our loved ones and kinder to each other. This is the only thing we can really do, and it is the most important.

Student: My first question is: at which level of realisation does someone need to read the Tibetan Book of the Dead, in order to benefit the person dying? And the second one is: what is your advice to do at the moment of death?

Rinpoche: Usually you don't need to have a certain level of realisation in order to read the Tibetan Book of the Dead. It is said, that it is better if it is read in the home of the person who died by someone in whom the dead person had lots of confidence. So the more the person who has died trusts the person who reads it, the better it is for that person. It is not necessary for the person reading to have high realisation. But the person who does the Phowa has to be highly realized if possible.

All that I said before is actually advice for the person who is dying. I think the most important thing is not to be too afraid, because fear is very painful. It is very destructive because you panic. It brings up lots of suffering and frustration and also many negative emotions as well. So it is no good at all. There is no need for fear and panic. We must understand as deeply as we can that the best thing to do is to have a peaceful state of mind in the face of death, a mind as clear and positive as possible.

This is said to be the main thing at the time of death. This is true at any time but especially at the time of death. If you can focus your mind on something more positive that would be very good. Therefore, all the different kinds of religious and spiritual traditions have their own way of expressing this. For example, if you believe in God you pray to God; if you believe in any master or saint or whatever, maybe Buddhas and Bodhisattvas, you focus on that. Something that you feel as positive, it doesn't actually matter what it is. There is a story in Tibet which is important in many ways. It is said that one Khampa (a bit like a cowboy, but from Eastern Tibet) was dying, and a Lama was brought to help him. The Lama said, "You are about to die, so think about Amitabha Buddha, think about your Lama and the land of Dewachen." Dewachen is Buddha Amitabha's paradise and it is said to be easy to be born there. The dying man said, "This doesn't come to my mind." The Lama asked, "What comes to your mind?" "The only thing that comes to my mind is sizzling sausages," the man answered. In Tibet there is this kind of sausage that you heat it up in the ashes of a fire and it comes out hot and covered in ash. It is delicious! So the man said, "I can only think of that." This Lama said, "Oh yes, that's very good! In Dewachen, on every tree these sizzling sausages grow. You just have to open your mouth and the sausages fall into your mouth. Even the Buddha there is little bit ash-coloured. Can you think about that?" "Yes," the man said, "I can think about that." So he died focusing on the sizzling sausages. That's the idea, it is not so much the sizzling sausages, that is just a funny example or story, but if we can focus our mind on something positive like compassion, wisdom, or anything that represents that, it is very good for a person to die in this way.

Student: My question is, I have a couple of friends who have committed suicide, and what I've read is that people who have committed suicide become disembodied beings. I would like to clarify this with you. What does actually happen in these cases, and is there anything I can do to actually help them?

Rinpoche: Usually from a Buddhist point of view, to commit suicide is like taking a life. Therefore it is not good. When you commit suicide, you are usually in a negative state of mind. You are angry or very sad, upset, or desperate. So when you die in that state, it is not very good because you will not be dying in a positive state of mind. You are usually concentrated on negative things. But, of course, you can't generalise too much. It varies from person to person and also it depends on the particular situation. Lots of people committed suicide during the Chinese invasion of Tibet. Many people committed suicide because they couldn't bear the pain. In my own monastery in Tibet, 14 monks committed suicide because they were being tortured. So people who commit suicide are usually going through very serious problems that they cannot face, or cannot see a solution. It is a desperate situation for them. It's very important if we can help people in those situations, in order to help them change their minds. Sometimes people call me and say they want to commit suicide but then we talk for a while and they don't commit suicide. It might be that they are not able to see their problems clearly and it helps them to talk to someone and maybe see a different perspective.

In the Buddhist tradition we have special practices for people who have died. For example, introducing them to the nature of mind, teachings to bring their consciousness back and practices to show them the way through. There are many different kinds of practices and empowerments. The purpose of all of these is to help. Of course the people who do these things must have compassion and, if possible, some realisation. This is especially important for people who have died an unnatural death. There are specific practices for that. But generally I think any kind of positive action done and dedicated to anyone who has died will help them.

Student: This has been very emotional for me. I've actually come from a funeral and I'm feeling quite emotional. It has also brought back a lot of very painful feelings of loss. My little brother died a few years ago and I don't really know what to do with that pain. I want to shut it off, I just want to go and watch television or do anything not to face it. These thoughts are like somebody else was saying, "Okay, impermanence, that's fine, I understand that." And then I start thinking in my mind about him dying. It goes around and around in my mind in a very negative way, and I wondered if you had any suggestions or any particular practice I could do. I can see that I am still very attached to my brother. I miss him and I'm very attached to him. The feeling has resurfaced today.

Rinpoche: When you lose somebody you love, I don't think you completely get over it. That's my experience. It becomes better in a way, after many years. But that's the fact of life. It has always been and always will be like this. We are born, we live our life and then we die. Some die earlier, some later. We must understand that deeply. It is not certain that my children or somebody else I'm close to will not die tonight. It's not certain that I will not die tonight. Tonight could be my last night. But it's not very useful to me or anyone else to feel bad just because of that. Life is so short and we cannot waste it feeling bad. There's no time to feel bad because who knows whether I will see tomorrow or my death first. That is the understanding. One day follows another and I must try to find some way to bring a kind of balance and peace to myself. Whatever happens I must prepare for death. I must feel a sense of urgency for myself. The more I am prepared, the more I think I can also help others. This understanding, this experience, is very important. We have all lost near and dear ones and we know we could die at any time. The time we have now is very precious but things could change quickly at any time. Therefore, the little time we have now cannot be wasted in just feeling bad or worrying or fighting with our near and dear ones. We must really make the most of this time we have with our loved ones, in the nicest way possible. We should try to be joyful and use this time in a more pleasant and positive way. We must learn how to feel good, how to find peace. To find peace within myself should become a very high priority, not only because it is important for our death, but also for our life and for all time. This attitude is the main thing, the most important thing. If we believe in another life continuing after this one, that we will be together once again with those we love at some point or another. Then we know that we can never be totally separated from them because of karmic connections.

Student: Could you please speak a little about the phenomenon of clairvoyance. In particular, as it is said that after the consciousness has moved away and left, it can be contacted by others. Could you speak a little about that?

Rinpoche: Now, the understanding from the Buddhist point of view is that because the nature of our mind is awareness and clarity, it has the capacity to know beyond physical boundaries. Our mind has the capacity to be clairvoyant; it has a capacity to be almost omniscient. That's what they say, and this capacity is also reflected in our intuition and things of that nature. It varies from person to person. When somebody is highly realised and can go into very deep meditation, and possesses certain karmic tendencies, they can see dead people, or the consciousness of other people. That's how it is understood, but here is a story:

Milarepa, the great and famous yogi, had many students. He also had a student whose parents were Bonpos. When he passed away, his other students asked of Milarepa what had happened to him: where had this student gone? Milarepa said he had gone to Dewachen, the paradise in the west. Then the Bonpos did some rituals for some time, as was usual. But then, the consciousness of the dead person seemed to come back. The consciousness came to a medium and it spoke of many things. It seemed he was really present there, and many people were confused. They went to Milarepa and said: "You said your student has gone to Dewachen, but it doesn't seem to be true because he is here according to this medium. He comes and talks and knows about everything. How can this be?" Milarepa said: "Okay, next time he comes you should ask him one question. Ask him, what is the secret name that Milarepa gave him when he received the empowerment." So they went away, and when this person's soul or consciousness came to the medium they asked of it, "What was the secret name that Milarepa gave you when you received the empowerment?" The voice seemed a bit worried and said "No, no,

I was not allowed in there. I was driven out of that compound. I wasn't there." And then the consciousness left. Milarepa said there are lots of spirits who pretend to be dead people, because they know all about most people from their past. So they appear and tell you they are this or that person. This is their profession, their hobby. There is a kind of being who does that. So, just because some 'thing' says it is this or that person you should not accept and believe this, it may not be true.

Student: Rinpoche, this might seem like a very stupid question, but I'm interested to hear your answer. In the West they say once you get to 40, 50, 60 or 70 it's too late to change, you can't change. But Rinpoche, is it ever too late to work on one's habitual tendencies? This is my question.

Rinpoche: No, I don't think it's ever too late. I've yet to start, but I'm going to start from tomorrow! Actually, from the Buddhist point of view, habitual tendencies are always there. It's not that when you are a baby or a small child you don't have habits. You are born with your personality, and also with your habits. And this can be seen very clearly when you see babies. I have seen lots of babies because I have many nieces and nephews. You can see that each and every one of them is totally different. They do not come into the world with a completely clean slate. They come with fully-fledged emotions, reactions and habitual tendencies. They come with personalities. It is all there. Of course when you are younger it's easier to learn things like languages, and many other things you can learn more quickly. But I think you can learn when you are older also, especially as changing habits is not like that kind of learning, it is slightly different. It is not just intellectual learning; mind learning is more like heart learning, and I think that can happen anytime.

Student: I was thinking mainly about working on one's mind.

Rinpoche: Yes I think that can happen, maybe it is even better if you are a little more mature. The older you become, the better it is. Why not?

Student: A week today my dearest dog died and my greatest wish is that it may attain rebirth as a human. I just wanted to ask you how animals can attain birth as a human, what do they have to have done in their life?

Rinpoche: There is a saying in Tibetan. It goes like this: 'Before you are born as a human you are born as a dog, before you go to hell you become a politician!' I hope there are no politicians here. So maybe your dog will become a good human being, but of course you can also say prayers and do other things and do the dedications on its behalf.

Student: Rinpoche please can I ask you for your thoughts on this. You have talked about trying to live your life showing as much love and compassion towards your loved ones and other people around you during the short period of time our life lasts. I understand also what you said about life being a cycle of birth and death on a daily basis. Basically, we talked about the actual death and the after-death experience. But when people have spent years in their advanced age, and they physically and mentally change in front of us, they physically deteriorate and they lose their lucidity and clarity of mind; maybe they are in constant pain for years and years and they can sometimes become hindrances. We become irritable and impatient in dealing with them, in spite of our best efforts. What advice can you give to us to always remember that one day we will become old and feeble, and that we too would like people to become compassionate towards us? What can we actually do so as not to lose patience and continue to give this kindness, love and compassion, even when it is for a long period of time?

Rinpoche: Yes that is right, life is like that. We are all very dependent on each other. When we are born we are totally dependent on other people, we can't do anything for ourselves and the people who look after us have to be extremely patient, no? Otherwise it is not possible to survive. And not just for one or two years. Sometimes it is more like twenty years that parents look after their children. And then, sometimes, they leave in an angry way! It is even more difficult then, isn't it? Somebody you have raised with all your kindness and all your patience, with all your expectations and love, they go away without even thanking you. This happens many times and I think that's very sad.

Also, when we are sick, whether young or old we depend again completely on other people. When we become old it is almost like we become a child again. When you are sick and young you can become strong again, but when you are old you become more and more like a child. That's the way it is. Sometimes people want to live very long, but living too long may not be so good in some cases. There are people who retain a very clear mind and they remain independent into their eighties. But also there are those who deteriorate very rapidly. This varies of course, from person to person. We all know people in these different situations. So, I think it's very important and a very positive thing to do, to be the kindest we can be, to do the most positive things we can do and to be of help to the old. For old people there is usually no getting better. Therefore, I think it's even more necessary to be patient and kind towards them. Not always easy, as you say, but nevertheless very important.

Thank you very much.

Glossary

Amitabha Buddha : The Buddha of Infinite Light.

Bardo : The intermediate state between the end of one life and rebirth into another. Bardo can also be divided into six different levels; the bardo of birth, dreams, meditation, the moment before death, the bardo of dharmata, and the bardo of becoming.

Bonpo : A follower of the indigenous shamanistic religion of pre-Buddhist Tibet.

Dalai Lama : The exiled spiritual leader of the Tibetan people.

Dewachen : The Pure Land of Amitabha, also known as Sukhavati: 'The Land of Bliss'.

Dharma : In Buddhism, the word Dharma refers to the teachings of the historical Buddha, the spiritual path to which his teachings are a guide, and the true nature of reality. Knowing the Dharma is more than simply being able to recite Buddhist texts: it is having the experience of the Buddhist path and gaining clear insight into the true nature of reality.

Dilgo Khyentse Rinpoche : (1910-1991) Acknowledged as a peerless master of the Dzogchen teachings.

Gampopa : (1079-1153) Milarepa's greatest disciple. Founder and holder of the first monastic Kagyû Lineage.

Jataka stories : A collection of stories of the previous lives of the Buddha Shakyamuni before he became the Buddha.

Kagyu : One of the four main lineages in Tibetan Buddhism. The others are : Nyingma, Sakya and Gelug. The Kagyu lineage originates from the primordial buddha Vajradhara and is passed down from master to student. The forefathers of the Kagyu lineage are the Indian mahasiddhas Tilopa and Naropa whose student, Marpa the translator, brought the lineage to Tibet.

Kalpa : A Sanskrit word meaning aeon or long period of time.

Kalu Rinpoche : (1905- 1989) One of the great Tibetan masters of our times. He was one of the first Lamas to teach extensively in the West and has founded many of the first Dharma centres there.

Karmapa : The head of the Karma (Kamtsang) Kagyu lineage (see: Kagyu). A line of reincarnated lamas from the first Karmapa Dusum Khyenpa (1110-1193) to the present head of the lineage, His Holiness the 17th Karmapa Orgyen Trinley Dorje, born in 1985. His predecessor was the 16th Karmapa Rangjung Rigpe Dorje. 'Karmapa' means "the one who carries out buddha-activity" or "the embodiment of all the activities of the buddhas".

Kham : A region in Eastern Tibet.

Khampa : An inhabitant of Kham. Khampas are said to be very brave and good horsemen.

Lhasa : The capital of Tibet.

Mahayana : 'The Great vehicle', the school of Buddhism which lays down the altruistic Bodhisattva path. The other two vehicles of Buddhism are Shravakayana (sometimes called Hinayana, 'The Lesser vehicle') and Vajrayana.

Marpa : Marpa Lotsawa, or Marpa the Translator (1012-1097) was responsible for conveying the mahamudra teachings from India to Tibet. He was born in the southern part of Tibet known as Lhodak. The wealth of yogic and mahamudra teachings he gathered, mastered and translated, were transmitted in their entirety to Jetsun Milarepa.

Milarepa : Jetsun Milarepa (1040-1123) is Tibet's most revered poet-saint. His whole-hearted commitment to the spiritual path, and his subsequent attainment of supreme enlightenment in a single lifetime, have been a source of spiritual inspiration to generations of Tibetans.

Naropa : (1016-1100) A great Indian scholar, chief disciple of Tilopa and guru to Marpa.

Phowa : A Tibetan term for a Buddhist meditation: 'transference of consciousness at the time of death'.

Sakyapa : An order of Tibetan Buddhism, there are four schools, Gelugpa, Nyingma, Kagyu & Sakya.

Shunyata : "Emptiness" or "Voidness", is a characteristic of phenomena; impermanent nature of form means that nothing possesses essential, enduring identity. In the Buddha's spiritual teachings, insight into the emptiness of phenomena is an aspect of the cultivation of insight.

Vajrayana : (Tib. dorje tegpa) The 'Vajra Vehicle'. Began in India but exists most fully in the Tibetan Tradition. The practice of taking the results as the path.

Dedication

All my babbling,
In the name of Dharma
Has been set down faithfully
By my dear students of pure vision.

I pray that at least a fraction of the wisdom
Of those enlightened teachers
Who tirelessly trained me
Shines through this mass of incoherence.

May the sincere efforts of all those
Who have worked tirelessly
Result in spreading the true meaning of Dharma
To all who are inspired to know.

May this help dispel the darkness of ignorance
In the minds of all living beings
And lead them to complete realisation
Free from all fear.

Ringu Tulku

Other books by Ringu Tulku

HEART WISDOM SERIES:
- *No. 1 Mahamudra & Dzogchen*
- *No. 2 Ngondro, a Commentary*
- *No. 3 From Milk to Yoghurt*
- *No. 4 Like Dreams and Clouds*
- *No. 5 Dealing with Emotions*

THE LAZY LAMA SERIES:
- *Buddhist Meditation*
- *The Four Noble Truths*
- *Refuge: Finding a Purpose and a Path*
- *Bodhichitta: Awakening Compassion and Wisdom*
- *Living without Fear and Anger*

Path to Buddhahood
Published by Shambhala

Daring Steps
Published by Snow Lion

Mind Training
Published by Snow Lion

The Ri-me Philospohy of Kongtrul
(In Tibetan but also published in English by Shambhala)

The Boy who had a Dream
An illustrated book for children
available from Rigul Trust at
www.rigultrust.org

IN OTHER LANGUAGES:

Finnish:
- *Turvapaikan ottaminen*
- *Elämä ilman pelkoa ja vihaa*
- *Mielenharjoitus*

French:
- *Et si vous m'expliquiez le Bouddhisme*

German:
- *Das Juwel des Drachen: Maerchen aus Tibet*
- *Der Lazy Lama betrachtet die Buddhistische Meditation*
- *Der Lazy Lama betrachtet die Zuflucht:Sinn und Pfad*

Norwegian:
- *Buddhistik Meditasjon*
- *De Fire Edle Sannheter Om tilflukt. A finne et mal og en vei*

Spanish:
- *La Meditacion Budista*

For an up to date list of books by Ringu Tulku, please see the Books section at

www.bodhicharya.org

All proceeds received by Bodhicharya Publications from the sale of this book go direct to humanitarian and educational projects because the work involved in producing this book has been given free of charge.